DITCHLAPSE / [REALLY AFRAID]

DITCHLAPSE

tommy wyatt

Querencia Press – Chicago IL

QUERENCIA PRESS

© Copyright 2024
tommy wyatt

ISBN 978 1 963943 90 0

Cover Image: Scott Webb

www.querenciapress.com

First Published in 2024

Querencia Press, LLC
Chicago IL

Printed & Bound in the United States of America

advance praise for DITCHLAPSE

tommy wyatt's writing ensures you get winded and wounded in this vivid recollection surrounding modern technology, identity, tragedy, and loss. right from the beginning, tommy's words guide you through their body and their personal tragedies, taken apart and meticulously inspected through the form of modern social media. *DITCHLAPSE* is the true amalgamation of the juxtaposition of tommy's selves: on media and in life. tommy's words ensure a crisis in *DITCHLAPSE's* readers, while furthering their own understanding of tommy, both as a poet and as a person. there is no limit to the level of understanding, tragedy, and identity crises that *DITCHLAPSE* induces upon its readers. *DITCHLAPSE* itself is best described as raw and visceral, and tommy does an absolutely amazing job conveying their emotions to their readers.

—arushi (aera) rege

DITCHLAPSE, in its pursuit of exploring the liminality of the digital world and the experiences of mental health issues, creates a liminal space in itself. A world in which infomercials play mid-poem, selling you a miracle cure, as you listen to your inner monologue replay some of wyatt's experiences as if they were your own. The poems trap you like you're doom scrolling late at night, forcing you to listen with expert craft of form and metre, like they're exploiting the algorithm of your brain. *DITCHLAPSE* is a tour de force of glitches, stutters, and pixel projections, that make you feel seen in your darkest moments, lit up by neon. It aches with the burden of internet culture—the good, the bad, and the stigmatised.

—Ozzy Welch, author of *Toothache*

The leading voice in tommy wyatt's *DITCHLAPSE* expresses a relatable sense of subservience to uncertainty. Each piece in the collection is a loop in itself, asking its audience to "unplug the TV ... before it consumes us whole." In these pieces, wyatt emphasizes what it means to be consumed. How a shadow can be so devastating. How a shadow can be the "parasocial love in the netherhours." In a collection so visceral, wyatt actualizes desire in its most digital form, describing a person being the self in self-destruction; the hidden figure in a figureless moment.

—Aldrin Badiola, editor-in-chief of *Artists from Maryland*

tommy wyatt is who you go to when you're in the mood to be delightfully blindsided by words like *spaghettification* and *gummyfried* in the middle of a harrowing identity suspension; when you want to know what it's like to live in TV static or haunted pools, munch on the crunchiest, immediately visceral descriptors, and connect with the unknowable—*DITCHLAPSE* will take you there. The titles come in hot, searing the stage for succinct poems that'll leave you with, as wyatt concludes in one poem, the "need to sit with that for a moment." This is perhaps some of wyatt's best stuff. Or at least, it's my favourite, and I think? at this point I've read all their stuff.

—vale prosper, 1/2 the writing duo for *Your Servant, Mephistopheles*, and a scattered dozen other poems around the globe

CONTENTS

please note the following subjects are explored in the text:
dissociation, self-harm, sleep paralysis, nightmares, and night terrors

DO NOT RESUSCITATE

clawing out of a coffin bareknuckled / haze of insulation pink / body pockmarked with wounds tripping trypophobia / bloodfluxing from jellied and friable tissue / materials mucked up for architectural disaster / how it's a design flaw / the graveyard misting with sawdust / as i ply my hands / through the fresh slab of dirt

what if we consider the cemetery to be a rigged claw machine instead / how everything is supposed to be glazed / over in feral and pungent yellow light / how it gives tangible static as a migraine / ribbed with chromecold / the illusion is how it makes me feel / alive / when i'm chosen with *shnnnng!* certainty / by someone else's hand

and i just have to ask / why do i keep coming back?

YOU SAY I'M DELULU FOR EXPLAINING LEVELS OF DISSOCIATION

(b-movie titled "inside me, there are two wolves")

i've lived so many times and i'm tired
i'm not even joking but does it even

matter when i dissociate from laughter
like lol the vibes are all wrong

in a "i've been here before" way
colorized in faeriegreen absinthe

breakfast of champions that makes me
want to go back to sleep and see more

time altered by dreamcloven skies
how their blank white clouds

wheel on like vhs film
be kind rewind

right? see how my skin reels
with spectral sheerlight

and i know it's too soon
to be softened and blearing

my body liquidshimmying
to faint rainblue fuzziness

particles in the condensation
of twilight. yes, time skipped

again and i am howling
because it's so fucking funny.

GESTURES BROADLY AT EVERYTHING

so blankstricken, so *bored now*

in quartz pink, pinching my skin

all in the consequence of need

to be more ghost than person

let me be nowhere

let me close my eyes

absorbed by a glitzing aura

so i don't blink,

to exist on the other end

paralysis-kissed and ethereal

touched by sleep

just this once.

I THINK I'M MORE FINEMISTED GRANULES OF TIME THAN PERSON

sometimes i'm frozen almost, like pixelations submerged in AI-cryonics, in a forked shadows air so dimensional it sputters rain skydown, mist breaking terrain of vantablack void. i'm there, incubated, like the nightmared version of *Aliens*, waiting to be pruned as the puce twilight brandishes the days inn hotel room, summer misting yellow in crescentwaves of the TV, distorted by grayfisted static when vision clicks back into focus.

INTERDIMENSIONAL CABLE / TAGS FOR #UNCANNYVALLEY #MAKEUPTUTORIAL

my face in the mirror

is all crater, no features

stretching over cosmic bright flesh
plasticbound so tight my breath
shudderdogs in the form

of three dots plinking

gauzedgray to nothing

as i lipsync to trending sounds with millennial pause,
calibrated to the speed it takes to videotape
wool unraveling in claymotion

how my mouth balks at the air
when gaudy synths pinch

with tinnitus, i ask if you're afraid by now
my face pressed against crushed powder
grimacing for a 60-second delay

we interrupt our programming on

DITCHLAPSE NETWORK

INFOMERCIAL AS THE MOMENT RIGHT
BEFORE A FLASHBACK

nachträglichkeit
as a pocket
realm, packaged
like you can
purchase it
today, any time
of day or night!

missing
something

here's a tip for you

technical glitch, digitally
processed product: why is your
voice twisted inertia when you
pick up the phone, why risk delay
in sound when you can have it
before you even want it?
you need to click the dial tone on,
as ringing crinkles like it's

skipping?
do you see what it can do? how it
drifts through to rip you clean out,
its compressed telekinesis
on the line: keep waiting or turn
off the screen.

DLN   1-800-757-7777   (call now!)

back to our programming on

DITCHLAPSE NETWORK

IS THIS ANALOG HORROR OR ANOTHER NIGHTMARE?

when i move my body it's not even   mine,
just data on a terminal in the form of   me
choosing to explore   a rubypocked
metal staircase   in the dirtbruised
woods: its spiral   twinkling *pink!*green
phosphors, a neon   corrosive to dead
pixels pipeline,   right?   all things
end sometimes when   the wiring
is fried, simulations   running an image
on an image   of an image   of me
climbing these stairs   that reach
to the oblivion of sky   emptying
its color before it rains,   before
the almost existence of mist   is too
contaminating and the game   restarts
to vantablack blank, reflective in its nature.
there aren't any choices left   in the coding,
really there's   nothing at all
and i need to sit with that   for a moment.

TRIANGULATION

rain gouging sockets with bright cerulean,
chemically induced tunnel vision, my eyes

like scythes. the body watches you tend
to these wounds with glittering gossamer,

how it expands like the spagettification
of static. why claim this moment is lagging

to the next when we've been past this
already? i glitch out, memory compressed

to corrupt. but you see me
throbbing with gelatinous rain,

clouds pumiced to cerebral blue. i know you
fetishize crying by demanding me to stop,

how i loosen to mist, how pounding it pours
from the skull of sky.

IPHONE IN RETROGRADE

airy swirling   whoozyquick

i don't have   any will

to yield   crushed by night

                               gummyfried and honeyed

to disorienting waves

                               buzzed with gray
                               i'm buffering

                               to exist

how to realize my potentialfuture after this? do i apply myself to online places so ditchlapsed to repeat the past where i am blankscreened and frightened by a pocket of steely blue oxidized and dulled. would you look how it wields us well? why try to alter what works, what's really in my hands right now?

YOUR APPROACH AS THE AVERAGE PERSON IS A SELF-DIRECTING CREDIT?

crying without tears is so clearpilled and angelgirl chique, like how could anyone think you did anything? like, you're so *genuine* in a way that rhymes with whine. why say it with your throat grinding russet light, dustfilled? want me to watch how it billows out to the lack of sky in a no-frills, woodslabbed panels? did you say the background was a rental?

watch your mouth puffing more air out than anything heartfelt. i mean, let's be real. are you: *filibustering*, *lovebombing*, or *so true bestie?* why do you need me to see you in such dismal light, saying sorry as you pinch your eyes into stars, thinking you have any luck convincing me you miss me at all? that you're so sickstung by love for me you had no choice but to tell me through filmstunk screens on your iPhone 13 because even the police said you had to leave my property? i don't know how you hold it together, pretending to be on the painbrink of denied existence like the rest of us.

how it makes you blink those bluesky eyes one more time! why are they so fucking dry?

TEMPORAL CELEBRITY

starfished on poolwater
    i'm doomdreaming the sun
this doesn't feel like
    freezestricken is
how it shimmers
    call it
greened out
    because
and whose will is it
    like déjà vu
of temporal celebrity
    to be anywhere else
me another letter
    to whose will is it
in such liminal structures
    what haunting strictures
a costume of body
    i don't need it
and how can you ask

malachite misting
    misses me this time
floating when it should
    the body
from shifting light
    ghostswimming
with glitterglam
    nothing else matters
to be here
    disguised as a vacation
aura's too bright this time
    so why don't you write
fleeting flashes back
    to keep me here
of sunken guilt
    can do but make
the skin wasting to foam
    but what of you

who's really   alone?

we interrupt our programming on

DITCHLAPSE NETWORK

INFOMERCIAL AS THE MOMENT
RIGHT BEFORE A FLASHBACK

If you just saw *Perfect Blue,* feeling devoid of

apparition gray

craving for more works of cyberstalking?

look no further

deepfakes wrinkling over you, like where you costume your body of choice with waveform luminance at a second delay!? it's only patchwork for our analog style to update. please connect to a terminal at the computer café, parasocial love in netherhours

does it twitch between your legs?

to become the object of your desire, start a webpage, upload your assumed form, press send to that special someone.

DLN   1-800-757-7777   (call now!)

back to our programming on

DITCHLAPSE NETWORK

MIRRORSELF

am i more vortex or spirespeckled screen,
why ask when i'm afraid of admitting
to anything that distends to static
in gunmetal gray, so blankcortexed
and fizzling out like late night programming—
an expanse of nothingness colorized by the faintest
of blues, pewter grains scrunching the edges.
something is missing, don't you think?

[please don't hurt me.] shudders through closed captioning
when you least expect it. you know i'm stuck in a freeze
response right now when you're dissecting this dialogue
out of context, but i need you to unplug the tv. bash
the screen blitzing to black, swallow fistfuls of glittering
glass and ribbed metals before it consumes us whole.

TIKTOK CLOWN ASMR

selling flashlights on TikTok shop

cake on coquettish eyeliner in teardrop style
tinny crunching as flakes crydown

the screen staticprickled
if i swipe lightly over the timestamp

to when you twist whispers, spitting out cherry pits
or plucking air out of the chasmblue,

flicking on a brighfluxed flashlight
to follow with my eyes. and it worked, you know,

because i open my drafts to a rough edit of me
caking on angelwhite eyeliner in teardrop style,

flakes crydown and crunch a tinniness,
chrome spheres glittering when i blink

with enough pressure, drifting off to cryptic
dreams that pluck me out of time,

and you?

I REALLY WISH I COULD CRY RIGHT NOW

somewhere there are negatives of me possessed by sleep paralysis, my legs bent over the edge of the bed, starpocked mattress exposed by flash.

i'm dreaming about falling, and i don't know why. i'm dreaming to pass the time. i'm dreaming in endless cyancrashed skies, how there's nothing i can do

but see how each image triples with apparitions, how my body is thrice posed, now with angelic proportions? so many legs, it looks like i've learned how to run.

THE INTERVIEW

you: wanted to be static and not a flesh suit all hooven, cubed with sweat, tell

me: a bit about it? be a better person, if you wish? why don't you tell me how you really feel? be loose with honesty again, promise it will save

you: from no life ever led, only tended in dreams, how it texturized daytime sound at 10% opacity, in dreadgreen or some other metaphor to choose, to talk about

me: as if i, too, switch truth for jester-trocities of the body horror variety? but i guess i can't blame

you: if it's the only tool you've had to survive, should've known sooner how blitzed the image of you really is in a third dimensional space. forgive

me: for this, but did you mean to mend when you're rendered so frayed and grizzled gray?

~TOMMY'S ROOM~
AS A TIKTOK LIVE

TikTok live as a simulated wasteland
of longing: the fake background breaking
to spirals of woozy, purplish blue. I turn
over in my sleep, pixels of exposed breast
crashing into frame as the rasp in your voice
winds to a scratchy minor C, asking: "Can I live
rent free in your mind?" The audio distortion
is dreamified as arms suffused with screenbright
warmth, their tactile static shaking me
into the oblivion of my phone where light
pulls an astralghost out of me. Your comments
read: "Is that your bed? Are you all alone
in that room? Can I see you soon, see more
of you?" You're my top viewer, my only viewer,
really, and you want me to be perfect for you,
even as I short-circuit out of vision. You speak
again: "I do now, if I don't already." My body
stirruped and baresplayed in a way you
could digitally erase the crinkly purple top sheet
and anything else on me, anything you want.

Thank you to the editors and publications who originally homed these poems:

- "do not resuscitate" in Bullshit Lit
- "is this analog horror or another nightmare?" in fifth wheel press
- "*~tommy's room~* as a TikTok live" in Fatal Flaw

This book contains references to *Buffy: the Vampire Slayer*, *Perfect Blue*, and Magdalena Bay's *Mercurial World*. The poems are also in mediation with *We're All Going To The World's Fair*, TikTok lives, TikTok ASMR, and infomercials from cable to TikTok.

Thank you for your support and championing this book:

Emily, nat, Sierra, arden, aera, vale, and Aldrin. Thank you to my partner and cats for warm nights of slumber and kindness.

tommy wyatt (he/they) lives with his boyfriend and their fiendishly goofy cats. he's the author of NOW THAT'S WHAT I CALL HORROR!; *So, Who's Courage?*; *TASEREDGED (watch out!)*; *Trick Mirror or Your Computer Screen*; *moviemotion*; and others.

[REALLY AFRAID]

tommy wyatt

Querencia Press – Chicago IL

QUERENCIA PRESS

© Copyright 2024
tommy wyatt

ISBN 978 1 963943 90 0

Cover image: Maghradze

.

www.querenciapress.com

First Published in 2024

Querencia Press, LLC
Chicago IL

Printed & Bound in the United States of America

for late night hauntings

lachrymose is a synonym, or is it a symptom?

a night of one act plays

contents

"lachrymose // lacuna", a series of one-act plays
review of CYOA

**A REVIEW FOR FANS OF *SKINAMARINK* (dir. Kyle Edward Bell),
BUFFY: THE VAMPIRE SLAYER (dir. Joss Whedon), *VERTIGO*
(dir. Alfred Hitchcock), & *MIDSOMMAR* (dir. Ari Aster)**

Life for TOMMY is always a vacation, the kind plagued by liminal space, a
beach full of strangers or NPCs in a simulation:
(whichever is easier to illicit *conviction*).

(The dustyred curtain is pulled by rope to two sides.)

TOMMY sits in front of the biggest box TV he's ever seen. The fuzzy screen
emitting a muted aquamarine, TOMMY'S eyes blink and still see blue-to-gray-
to-blue waves until everyone else is asleep.

Well, almost everyone. With his sisters kicking the sheets down and his mom
snoring sickeningly loud [...] *Yes*, they did wake TOMMY'S dad, who flicks on
an actual channel to a horror classic, that TOMMY will only recall as gestation
chambers or weird tubes of aliens morphing into nakedladies, TOMMY'S
pupils blink heavy like wet glue, or something else only eyes can feel.

(The curtain abruptly closes.)

(A projection of a row of motel rooms with the same nausea-induced vertigo
from an image pasted over and over on the washed out light—consider how
the filters are meant to look like a VHS tape but they're just cheap spiral
bokeh[...].)

CYOA

scene 1: SWIMMING OR A BAPTISM?

TOMMY'S body plunges in water, clumping from sudden warmth in the otherwise plumcold pool. Deep green algae clamp down on TOMMY'S throat to really sell a drowning scene.

When TOMMY surfaces, he must not fuss. (TOMMY must react touched; however that looks—perhaps imagine the best birthday gift.) For it only happened to his vessel, and the corporeal realm fluxes in a flush of time, long or short enough to ferment the spirit and return with a promise.

TOMMY breaks through as the sun beams, crushing a cluster of shadows. TOMMY cries, forgets to commit *be not afraid* to memory. What returned with TOMMY?

CYOA

scene 2: AFTER SCHOOL SPECIAL

Daydrunk on Nyquil, TOMMY'S brain is liquified and glazed with iodine blue, much like meat at a barbeque. Or, metaphorically, if it shakes just enough, it'll produce cryptic answers in absolutes: *Yes, No, Ask Later.* What will TOMMY do?

(This is the part when the play becomes a directorial choice. Choose carefully.)

A.   TOMMY kicks back and flicks on the TV, sitting as close to the screen as possible, eyes glowing with polygongreen. In 60 FPS, the cubed pixels sway to a loading screen. TOMMY clicks on the profile with 16 heart pieces. To avoid the Water Temple, TOMMY skips across Hyrule Field in leased daylight, the grass stagnant and piercing like chlorine. Later, TOMMY tells his sister he saved Zoras drowning under the drawbridge to Castle Town. TOMMY had to say something, and it had to be something good, or else TOMMY might not get to play again.

B.   TOMMY chats with a friend on AOL Messenger until his sister needs the landline. Funny enough, his sister will later call her boyfriend, who's telling TOMMY he's too old to play video games. Bequeathed it a "child's idle", and TOMMY idolizes the fuck out of his sister's boyfriend. But, it's okay. Boys play other things, often with themselves or, if luckstruck, with maidens. TOMMY receives one last message: a task to advance to the next level. And, it's a date.

CYOA

scene 3A: FREE PLAY: MERMAIDS

TOMMY is one of the few still too scared to swim even in the shallow end. He considers the rope separating each end to be an electric fence, lined with barbs and shards of sharp objects. But, it's the last class of the season. It coincides with his birthday. *Surprise!* TOMMY'S friend tackles him by the ankles underwater, TOMMY'S head smacking the rope.

FRIEND
You didn't pick a special power! That means I win.

TOMMY
(Choking back chlorine, TOMMY is too stunned to speak.)

TOMMY'S friend swims circles around him until he's dizzypulled by the artificial currents, spinning with animated stars (the kind that are sootgrey and have negative HP impact, think ztars from any Mario title).

FRIEND
(Laughing.)
Isn't it bizarre how you always lose, no matter what day it is?

TOMMY
I don't want to play mermaids with you anymore. You promised! (TOMMY cries. He's always crying. That's why it doesn't matter.)

FRIEND
TOMMY wants his mommy, TOMMY wants his mommy!!

The whistle blows out their ears. TOMMY is saved, but by what means? TOMMY must choose to tell the truth, in which case his friend will sorely lose.

CYOA

scene 3B: LITTLE DANCE, LITTLE DATE

TOMMY'S skin glitters from a computer screen flickerflashing and screeching like a 200-beats-per-minute-human-male laugh, yeah like Boo from *Super Mario*.

FRIEND
Frick, did it crash? C'mon, Tommy!

TOMMY
(Joltyjumps a couple inches in the air, hovering what feels like forever a moment too long.)
I did what you asked! (*Defensive. Why?*)

FRIEND'S BROTHER/TOMMY'S SISTER'S BOYFRIEND
(Investigates the room and finds a loose plug.)

FRIEND
(*Laughs.*)
What's wrong with you? (*Jokingly.*)

TOMMY
(Chokes back words.)

Now, TOMMY'S skin shines so bright so fake like glitter popping out of a balloon at a surprise birthday party, shines the airiest paleblue-to-gloomauve from a homemade movie.

TOMMY
I watched it.
(The words almost manifest out of TOMMY'S mouth.)

The video plays back, titled: *Playing Mermaids.*

FRIEND pins TOMMY to the bed, the mattress floating on water, and could easily put him in a chokehold. Now's not the time for that. Instead, FRIEND dips down, wethot breaths dripping on TOMMY's mouth.

FRIEND
See, isn't this fun?

(The tape's quality is degraded from scratchmarks, enjoy the pixelated-or-dreaming lighting.)

FRIEND'S BROTHER/TOMMY'S SISTER'S BOYFRIEND
(*Off-Screen.*)
What, are you gonna kiss, or something?

TOMMY goes limp and doesn't resist (it's not a choice when this little dance, little date is ritual, play for the real thing?). FRIEND spits on their lips and drowns TOMMY.

"lachrymose // lacuna", a series of one-act plays
review of THE VACATION

A REVIEW FOR FANS OF *SKINAMARINK* (dir. Kyle Edward Bell), AND
NON-FANS OF *BUFFY: THE VAMPIRE SLAYER* (dir. Joss Whedon),
VERTIGO (dir. Alfred Hitchcock), & *SLEEPAWAY CAMP* (dir. Robert
Hiltzik)

Life for TOMMY is always a vacation, the kind plagued by liminal space, a
beach or somewhere far enough from home:
(whichever is easier to illicit *conviction*).

(The dustyred curtain is pulled by rope to two sides.)

TOMMY sits in front of the biggest box TV he's ever seen. The fuzzy screen
emitting a muted grizzled brown, TOMMY'S eyes blink to waves, until
someone in the room thinks *is he gonna cry?*

Well, almost everyone. TOMMY'S dad flicks on an actual channel to true
crime to real life exorcisms to a horror "classic", where a child's corporeal
boundaries are at risk from "freaks", consumed by a freak who hates
transpeople. There's a connection to the viewer of choice here and one to the
viewer cornered by a single bed hotel room, king-style.

At the film's reveal, TOMMY'S pupils widen with yellow, pulpy masses heavy
like wet glue, or something else only eyes can feel. Starfished on the bed and
blankeyed, TOMMY remembers.

(The curtain abruptly closes.)

(A projection of a row of motel rooms with the same nausea-induced vertigo
from an image pasted over and over on the washed out light, and consider
how the filters are meant to look like a VHS tape but they're just cheap spiral
bokeh[...].)

THE VACATION

scene 1: DEEPCREEK, MARYLAND VACATION. 2009

AFTERNOON

TOMMY throws bait out onto the gelidglazed river from his dad's friend's yacht. All alone with the rickety fishing pole that can't cast for shit! The line is caught, but he doesn't wait before tossing it at full force. Now he's all bated breath and for what? The whole pole floats as indifferent ripples carry it so fucking slow. Was it really just to feel something?

TOMMY is too afraid to swim after it. Maybe he knows something we don't.

DUSK

The first time TOMMY cries listening to *Bubbly* fading to *Unwritten* is when he looks at his reflection after a steamwooled shower. His body still so limp from ick-in-the-throat feelings, the kind that tastes creamy going down. What is he remembering right now?

TOMMY doesn't say anything.

THE VACATION

scene 2: MYRTLE BEACH VACATION, NEXT YEAR

TOMMY listens to *27* by Fall Out Boy on his Bratz speaker (it's retrofitted in Sharpie because he's embarrassed he played with dolls, and still thought about playing with them, but sexuality was really confusing now) in the sunbaked car (the dust in a broken bokeh filter will shine just right in an intimate theater).

He leans onto the door, asleep. His slumber flickers the eyes, as the song clicks back to *Headfirst Slide Into Cooperstown on a Bad Bet* by Fall Out Boy. His nightmare will be dappled by "surfed out brain waves flick back and forth / like old headlights sniffing model glue again", as his mother lathers lotion in the front seat. His father quieted up for once, sucking in a cigarette for another patch of movement for the scene. (Think, this is more or less a homework assignment more than an actual one-act play. It's okay. There's always one.)

(As the curtain almost closes, TOMMY awakes. The lights flushed a clinical white on the stage.)

TOMMY stumbles into the room that fits a twin bed, takes the Days Inn pad of paper, and writes down the dream because it's the only thing that feels real these days. But the light is too bright, surgical in the way to conceal, and stitches over the words. Or does he just not want to say what it was? (This must be a clear deliberation for the audience.)

THE VACATION

scene 3: INT. OF A DREAM SEQUENCE IN TOMMY'S CLOSET (AT THE BEACH RESORT)

The walls are caked with emerald construction paper faded to a gross chartreuse, kind of like Mountain Dew baking in plastic under the smoldering sun. Harsh yellow glitter tape holds it all up in blotchy scrapes because TOMMY has to use his nails. Because TOMMY isn't allowed around scissors. It's burning hot outside, and *When It Rains* by Paramore blasts on a retrofitted Bratz boombox, which has been shaded over in splotchy black Sharpie. TOMMY's hands are clamping onto an iPod, sweat glazing the screen. TOMMY is texting on his iPod, using a fake phone number on a fake iPod-to-phone app.

CRUSH
So, why do you cut?

TOMMY
Because I want to be an open wound when I grow up.

CRUSH
I'm too afraid of blood.

TOMMY
No, not that hard. I press hard enough, but more like water pruning skin.

(Much later, TOMMY will find out how easy it is to slice through his corporeal form, how it feels like the impact of a chicken breast that isn't slippery. Consider this for an adaptation.)

CRUSH
Okay. Well, I don't trust that. How do you do it?

TOMMY cradles a dustcolored CD case in his hand, until the dullest jagged edges parse skin away just a little. It's not even a slit. The light goes out, synth clashing with dark. It doesn't feel good. It's more like that feeling TOMMY gets when he sucks skin off his lips, or plucks it off in desperate instances. Comforting in all the wrong ways.

FADE. INT. OF TOMMY'S BEDROOM.
TOMMY'S vision crashes with glassrefracted light, sun beaming through his windows. The light clasps TOMMY's throat, swallowing it whole, as he searches his body for marks. But TOMMY is packaged in blankwhite flesh, no scratches. Only ache.

THE VACATION

scene 4: NOT A CYOA MEMORY, SORRY KID

NARRATOR

You have a story, TOMMY. You almost died once. You hadn't eaten for days and woke in the lavatory, hazy with mist from the shower running, in heavyfluorescent whitebrightness. (Try to make it look like TOMMY is thinking about how he hopes he was any cast member from *Poltergeist* and, just maybe, would be cursed to die?)

(The lights go black for a moment, the projector flashes a starry sky. The night billows out as the lights fade back on.)

Yes, in that quick moment, you're strapped in the car, your eyes follow the road until it slopes to a sunshine logo'd motel. (Try to make it look like TOMMY is thinking about his last vacation. Was it his *last* vacation?)

You swallowed *Heaven* by Bryan Adams down like a spoke. Your eyes went bright, like cartoon stars when the dude's about to pass out from laughing at a good joke you don't understand. (The curtain, pittering, is an expression of time.)

What happened right then, when you went away? Would you call it a case of the strange and bizarre sudden loss of time? Would you call it a turgid evil festering in your body and call it sickness, or a concern for an exorcism? Is there really a difference when the pain possesses you? Or would you call it what it really is: dissociative black out? You'll stay, TOMMY. You'll wake up in vague lighting from your littledeath simulator corroding a mess of your vision.

TAKE THIS QUIZ!

11 QUESTIONS

TO SEE IF YOU AGREE WITH COURAGE AS A METAPHOR

contents

these poems have themes of parental abuse/neglect, medical trauma, asthma/chronic health conditions, bad/abusive relationship, sexual abuse

happy valentines day?
love, schadenfreude

holographic hearts on a valentine's card: *is it* 4th grade, when you tried to hide the hazy sun with your blanket even though there were scarier things to hide from,

is it much later when you're 14 and *socalled* unfeeling doctors are concerned about your pain more than anyone else whose only concern should be you and *if* you're in pain,

is it your monitor shattering the illusion to deadred pixels and you're in your midtwenties and you can't breathe and Peanut cries to find you while you tell your partner

how much it hurts and they make time to be with you through night that twists and churns in your throat and your AI chirping in its autotuned voice *this isn't normal*,

is it when you realize now that you hide so much fear and sick and pain from it all because you grew up believing it was fine your parents will always love schadenfreude

a lot more than you.

it is because it's never you.

who's afraid of feelings, anyway?

a whose line is it, anyway? meets *courage the cowardly dog* spin off episode
called "standup comedy of your nightmares"

oh my god why are teenage boys so afraid of feelings,
you complain about your soapy teen drama of the week,
into the void, into discord, until it becomes

disorienting in a drunk kind of way, where everything
is chartreusebruised as the sun shrivels it all up
and you're in the back room at your parents' house
with Him again and He shoved His fingers
into your lips, "so wet," His voice slurred
flat tones, kind of enjoying it especially by how
you're not even close.

and it's always and only a summer, an anniversary
where you uncover something uncouth, something too much, and what is
your plan as it compounds?

how would you feel? and would you admit it?

are you an internet cryptic? (as told by your tweets)

three wraiths appear before you:
    dr. pepper

are you:
      jittery & jolting & holding onto
      offerings that taste like cherry
      & notes of love: you know

sure:
        it can break on your tongue
        licks of spritz fizz a weirdwarm feeling
        but that's all it would ever do.

three wraiths appear before you:
    faith as a phase

maybe:
    god as a vice like self-flagellating
    to exact the pain, as a viper
    (it's giving mother)

maybe!:
    succession is suffering
    watch how you beg to break
    flesh packaged as delicacy
    stamped closed with threats?blessings?
    of "take this body!", taste it well after expiry

three wraiths appear before you:
neon yellow band-aids

maybe?:
      cut the bullshit when it all leads
      back to blanking on memories
      of the prayer circle at your pcp's office

and crying later in secret,
spiraling after drinking too much cherry
medicine, until you puke, until you exorcise
yourself, until you ask what is haunting
you now?

**hey, have you ever considered the word "rewind" may drop
from the next generation's lexicon?**

precursory questions

1. how many home videos did you keep?
2. how many seeped into adulthood, vhs tape wrinkled and blinking back at you the screen a reflection, skipping with white?

1.

your brain melting to squelchpink
as it zaps like pop rocks

on a sloppy wet tongue. Maybe
you were a person once?

ANSWERS:
A. except if you're lovesick and your face is sunken, even on valentine's
B. except you're 15-going-on-16 and afraid of sex and you learned
C. it's the only thing to fix you: except if you rewind
D. back to the first time, to crystal dolphins crashing off your nightstand
E. except you're only a kid, except anyone's wish is your command and that's why you're here, it's why you're always here

2.

where 2000s chrome futureblue dolphins
are common and evasive as glitter. the graininess
is so loud, wriggling
under your freshpressed top sheet. do you know

you're not even awake right now? can you guess
who's the voyeur and what they want with you?

ANSWERS:
A. who set the camera
B. who captures you
C. who extorts you
D. for your body, and pours stringy whitestatic in mouths. "open mouths are always hungry": you awake to this text message, sifting your recollection to glass, to fine grain.
E. and the graininess is so loud.
F. (all of the above)

who's afraid of feelings, anyway? (once more with...)

a *whose line is it, anyway?* meets *courage the cowardly dog* another spin off
episode called "standup comedy of your nightmares"

you hoarse your throat out
because you're breathing in specks
of light and frightened spit

until you experience attic chest,
yes, that annoying metaphor
teen poets obsess over and

throw in their poems
because they think it's pretty
because they really need it to be,

so, how are you 25-going-on-26?
needy to the point of dependence
because your parents failed you?

so needy that you feel
full of dust in russet light
again and again, that attic chest acting up

all the fucking way home,
to when you cry and
Peanut crying with you,

and who's the true Courage, anyway?
who's afraid of the unknown
and the known?

you never said your favorite color is green?

deep southern accents and bitingstiff peacock sofas
hum like sibilance in poetry, don't you think? you posed
in cowboy clothes when you were a baby, when everyone
hoped you'd be a boy, the image flickering pixels
dim to bright, and so they frightened you to be a girl,
humiliated by a typical Boomer L: digitalized as a Facebook post.
so, why'd you wear it as a disguise? you called it a *sorry excuse
of skin*. skin that bulged in a tight green swimsuit, in deep pools
under a yolkdrooping southern yellow sun. a vacation? it's always
a vacation. you remember this far back, so go deeper. *how
would it hurt*, you asked, asking your mom about death, because
you're sleeping over at your grandma's house (spoiler alert:
for the last time) where you're allowed to watch
Totally Spies and allowed to be in love with Clover
and bleeding heart flowers and deepgreen sky
in a watering can, and you're wondering what this all means
when you should really be wondering: where is Cosmo?

the physical exam, or an erasure?

in ███ distress.

reactive ███

and ███

tender ███

No

warmth

yields time.
No
deficit
normal.
This Visit
controlled
and
worsening ███ some
residual cough for ███ today.

Little interest

for the patient
to consent
without incident.

the physical exam,
or the interpretation?

the light so evasive, ingesting you like the void
and you guess it's harsh how the light arrests
your skin in sterilewhites.

you feel the moon swelling bigger than orange pocks
over a stretch of wisteria sky when the nurses
pin you down. don't you see it now, the faint moon
outside overlooking a church with tombs?

let the window bend vision with voidlight,
your eyes dry but reactive, as the nurse instructs you
to swallow the tube all the way it can go, saying:
"what a good, pretty girl!"

you throw up yellowsickle
vomit until the voidlight
swallows you whole.

like this review of Buffy the Vampire Slayer's S1EP10: "Nightmares"?

(or another reason to ask where is Cosmo?)

you are frightened by things
like dreams you're soon to
forget and disorient to texture
from the bright moon

or computer screen yellowed
by sickle light? your body's
topography unfolding like
paper like pixels like teeth in
privates to a grainy gray
beach to bodies in naked
spaces. you're where you
shouldn't be, aren't you?

still-imaged on His screen,
frightened by such things,
aren't you? by things like His
dreams? soon to forget,
aren't you?

textured moon disorients
you to your teeth, soon
sickened under sickle light
disorienting the most private
of beaches, so grainy and
gray, so naked in private
spaces, on private days,
that hurt all the same?

"rewind, what's that?" says every AI-generated uncanny valley level 'human' otherwise known as the next generation?

follow up questions:

1. how many seeped into adulthood, vhs
   tape wrinkled and blinking back at you
   the screen a reflection, skipping with white?
2. how many home videos did you keep?

(continued.)

1.

mostly A's mean... remember when he commanded you upstairs with the promise of something that will give you "cool status" and maybe act like you exist for once,

mostly B's mean... and so, did you trust him? twisting crystalchromed coded static in your eyes, your eyes excessively wet, squelchblinking so hard that you are a beam of light (or the screen flickering waves at night, or that

mostly C's mean... bright TriStar winged horse intruding and skipping and rewinding with white, with white, with white)—remember when he showed you, always inviting his sister, to gaze with you into the gummied haze of blood on an animatronic human-like doll like Chucky

mostly D's mean... from *Child's Play* (yes, you still can't watch it today) dripping down to your stomach again (yes, even then), chest pounding to an inverted star, and you feel something wrong, something adults in your life would say is unholy

mostly E's mean... and his touch browns your body with blood, leaving redhands on your body, flesh pounded to a star, and his sister hiding in the closet.

2.

or that bright TriStar winged horse intruding and skipping and rewinding (with white, with white, with white)—and you linger there, without further instruction.

eyes excessively wet, squelchblinking so hard that you're eating the grainy wheat background (or the beam of light (or the screen flickering waves at night

browned by blood or cherried crystals, he pulls blue dust from your cheeks, leaving flesh pounded on your body, redhands clicking from the alien sound of an indifferent cursor. what does the difference matter?

through the gummied haze of clowned, dripping down to your stomach again, flesh pounded out to an inverted star, clicking like a computer mouse and him? he's here now, everything

crystals pounding amethyst, blue dust pulls bust to blood eagle style: trust him. trust him? do you trust him, waking into dusk, your hands reaming

(This is Hell theory.)

you like another review: Skinamarink (dir. Kyle Edward Ball)?

[previously on tommy...]

an [adult swim]
april fools night slot

contents

these poems have themes of sexual abuse/assault, abusive friends, parental trauma, religious trauma, medical trauma, self-harm, suicidal ideation, death in the family

a review of so, who's courage (bullshit lit) [bumper]

you watched *courage the cowardly dog?* great. now listen—stop thinking about the things we do for love. consider: the things we do for fear (you're *so* close).

home movies or found footage? [bumper]

what else can you think about before time crashes on the shore, sweating all over you, the mist of memory bluing your skin like ice, like pepsi, and what if you remember what anything means? what could it really do when you were dry, too shy to try anything, even looking at yourself in a maze of mirrors at the department store? because if you look at yourself, you're projected out on your friend's mirrordoor closet? you're only sleeping over, you can wait it out a little longer.

don't worry how much the mosquitos bite at a night swim where you're forcedared to skinnydip "just a little bit", and alone with him? how old is he? thirteen, who threatens to know everything like he's god? and in blue shimmering tones splashing toward you, it's hard to see the difference. it won't take too long to dry in a summer night, shadows crashing all over you as he doubles in the things called nightshades he puts on your eyes. it's okay, you need to look away.

instead, ask yourself: what is the difference between the glare from metal stairs staggering in a mountain, appalachianstyle or the pair of fuzzy dice scarring your wrists with hairs of shadow? what are you doing calling speeding on the *highway after twilight descends over time* anything but a risk? sorry, a *calculated risk* assuming it's empty? what kind of dreamcore highway are you painting in this image? why does it have to look so pretty and cryptid when you don't know what you're all alone with?

a lie and a truth [bumper 1]

1. you're more time capsule than a person
2. you never thumbed a VHS, the tape reading: *be kind, rewind*

are you okay with the events currently unfolding? / what's the difference between a game from saw or a nightmare blunt rotation? [bumper 2]

why do you remember hearing your doctor saying something like he could perform a tracheotomy with a pen, and you really think your parents would let you go to him?

you're too young for your memory to be glittering with trauma. why else do you dissociate every time you "sleep over" at the hospital, the place you missed when your vision pittered off your bedroom, the walls bordered by vintage pastel teddy bears, or there'd be a risk, right—but whose risk? come on, remember it in punchdownpink, how you were in some cellar always pitched to night, and you always had a reason to be afraid?

wait, your mother's there now. and you will lose it when you're carried back (how's it feel to be a float in a parade?) to your room.

are you okay with the events currently unfolding? / what's the difference between a game from saw or a nightmare blunt rotation? [bumper 3]

remember when your doctor said something like he could perform a tracheotomy with a pen, and you really went to him? do you have a deathwish, kid? no, you won't be all alone, you're too young for that. no, really,

you're too young for that. why else can't you help but feel dissociated every time you "sleep over" at the hospital, the place you missed when your vision bounced off your bedroom, the walls bordered by vintage pastel teddy bears, or light pouncing, like a memory in punchdownpink? the place where there isn't night, so there isn't a reason to be afraid.

wait, *really*, that's it? your mother's there, though, starkserious as night. she knows you carved your body with safety scissors to be here. like, what's a little more pain after all, right? but what happens when the wound closes, when you survive?

remember when you picked out your grandma's coffin? [bumper]

what is the point of looking into a glass table, crashing your head through an artificial body that looks like you, or holographic shards of you? slobber pills from your mouth as you spin out of yourself. where are you now? enshrouded by forsythia, their fake-wet petals make you question everything at eight years old. you're losing the point again. this isn't why you've populated in a galvanized gray room, why you can feel the sting of the steel beams in your hands. stagger your breath for this unless you want to soak in your fears and ugly cry for real this time as you smell the faint freshcut bleeding heart flowers you culled from your grandma's garden. you asked why those flowers, pulling their sinewy wet from stem. she said they remind her of you, and you don't know what it means because you're only eight, so you think really hard about this now, and wonder about her favorite color. why is everything so disgustingly gray and gaunt and liminal? why are you questioning the wrong things again? look, you're only permitted to choose, make an executive decision at the table, sign your name below. so, you pick something pink. *good girl*, you hear, prompting you to ask: *can i pick out her dress, too?*

how to fish / how to feel fantastic [bumper 1]

you're freezing so hard you feel wet, rubbing the muscle of your pruned fingers together even harder you produce a mist. look at you now, collecting picks of your body's muckrain in a bucket.

now, say it with your chest: *luck has nothing to do with this.* seriously, please don't breathe so abruptly. the cold will crispcut pieces out of you, and you will not notice.

it's all in the wrist. loosen your cast and the fish will come to you is what you've been told all these years when, really, autotuned bubbles press in your ears, bursting backwards with song designed for nonhuman consumption. your chest crushed by congealed cold, fluid drumming in the throat.

how to fish / how to feel fantastic [bumper 2]

wriggling your body to a star in protest, just stop it. you're going fishing with dad. if you pitch a fit, you're a brat! now, that's enough, so what your vision is cut with deus ex machina? can't you leave the dissociation at home? just throw your garments in the bag and get on with it.

his hands so cold, *they pill with yellow* as he rolls a smoke to you: *if you ever feel like you want it, i will kill you, spear your body with a fishing rod. it's all in the wrist, and you will learn to listen.*

son of diesurrogacy, the fine line between fear and love, how will you respond? and what will he dissect from it, if not the daughter he props up like a paper doll from a miserly 2020s McDonald's Happy Meal, your eyes greasing over as you disintegrate to the freezing and unfeeling cold.

a series of voice recordings on your babyboyblue dsi, circa 2009 [bumper]

"kissing boys, girls? that's hot"
your voice warbling in a crackedmetal way at the end, *so* high, your best Paris Hilton impression. you know, the one you're five years late on. you think it's impressing your cool friends. what else do you say to *impress* them?

"courage the cowardly dog is gay"
did you not watch the hilary duff commercial, it's iconic? it's ironic (in the way your middle school self can understand the word "ironic"). lay the next one on me *champ*—

"why do i still have these pink BB pellets"
being socialized as a girl > desiring a gun > and other parts > in suburbia scarred by white sun > watch how you lunge > skinning on asphalt > all for your neighbor's BB pellets > who knew you'd take them > taunting: *pink is a girl's color anyway*

are you okay with the events currently unfolding? / what's the difference between a game from saw or a nightmare blunt rotation? [bumper 1]

you think time is a human glitch you think time is a human
how did you define *time dilation*, does it take
you think time is a human glitch you think time is a glitch?
anything at all to harness, or is it in the
you think time is a human glitch you think time is a human
wrist? (hah, did you take the bait,
you think time is a human glitch you think time is a glitch?
yeah, a joke barbed with a little spark,) now
you think time is a human glitch you think time is a human
how did you define it again? will
you think time is a human glitch you think time is a glitch?
you count yourself lucky you
you think time is a human glitch you think time is a human
can fist through your stomach (you don't need to try
you think time is a human glitch you think time is a glitch?
to either), with the same barb as a hook to
you think time is a human glitch you think time is a human
the ribs (easy like claw machines, huh), to stay
you think time is a human glitch you think time is a glitch?
awake through it? how are you really awake?
you think time is a human glitch you think time is a human

a lie and a truth [bumper 2]

1. you're an unreliable narrator
2. you never thumbed a VHS, the tape reading: *be kind, rewind*

is your favorite color blue or are you just sad to see me? / each time you go battery saver mode [bumper]

holographic brain matter spills from the body, the skull specifically. don't worry too much how long it takes to get to the point here. holographic brain matter spills from the body, the skull specifically. don't worry too much how long it takes to get to the point here. holographic brain matter spills from the body, the skull specifically. don't worry too much how long it takes to get to the point here. holographic brain matter spills from the body, the skull specifically. don't worry too much how long it takes to get to the point here. holographic brain matter spills from the body, the skull specifically. don't worry too much how long it takes to get to the point here. holographic brain matter spills from the body, the skull specifically. don't worry too much how long it takes to get to the point here. holographic brain matter spills from the body, the skull specifically. don't worry too much how long it takes to get to the point here. holographic brain matter spills from the body, the skull specifically. don't worry too much how long it takes to get to the point here. holographic brain matter spills from the body, the skull specifically. don't worry, don't worry how (forced) it felt.

stickerstars on the ceiling in their aliengreen gleam
paisley punctures of light on the floor
the air colorized in *Skinamarink* blue
do you know who was tasked with
watching you? sure, you were
two years old and afraid you
didn't know what you were
feeling, and it's okay to be scared
but it should only be sometimes.
and do you understand? the price it costs
to love you, your mother basically said? you
were too young to be told you didn't matter
and weren't deserving of basic needs because
it expended your mother's energy too much.
watching you. and in 20+ years, you'll read in your baby book
filled out until 1998 that one of the first sentences you ever
said was "*put me down!*" to your mother, who wrote:
*deadname hugged me for the first time at 10 ½ months old
(mom first)

when every birthday costumes itself a clown, a spirit halloween opens [bumper]

yes, you are *too much* when your reality destabilizes with
voidbass. there's a gash in the sound, it's moist and familiar.
it satisfies the way teething satisfies. once it breaks to lack,
you won't breathe any easier. if you stay here, you'll have to
play a pick-and-choose game that glitches at high frequency
with each play.

sad clown plush / red paint chips tattooing down the eyes / its broken teardrop staining white gloves / flecks scratchy and hoarse in the throat / its wind up distortion / sings a tinny cry / or a postautotune jump scare / it's your first birthday gift / you play 26 years later / still crushed in custard and amethyst / its tassel and hood / you want to climb into it / the only real things allowed to fuss / because you are its assigned caregiver / at 0 to now / how does it feel / to know / your birthday is always / a haunting / a lingering of the lack / it's okay right / you always come back / pull the childproof string / the plastic yellow handle / to distortionsong / something nightcore would sample / and you'd listen to it all the same

vibrant hued cesspool in green / brackish water / dungy sewer / a plume of smoke shoots / in the sky / the planted firework / the tricking only friends gift you / their hands pushing you closer / to the rusted grate / sweat thickening / greasing your leg to fit perfectly / *IT wants to eat you* / they sneer / holding back a laugh so well / you're begging them to stop / the sound obliterated / by private clouds / blaring sun yellowing your clothes / your crotch / but maybe that's piss / you aren't wearing underwear / and it's not a dream / maybe you should choose sleepovers / a bit more carefully next time / if there is one / after all / this clown may swallow you whole / with its zombie zested spatter of water / so close to skin / but it's all in good jest / the way your body buzzes / with the airiest bass / right before the beat drops

wow! this could be a david firth video [bumper 1]

your existence will be erased your existence will be erased
think back to swim class / how chlorine sickslicked in the
your existence will be erased your existence will be erased
throat / how you thrashed in water colder than an ice bath /
your existence will be erased your existence will be erased
how steam room air stares you down / makes you want to
your existence will be erased your existence will be erased
reconsider / if you want to be the reason for a blooper reel in
your existence will be erased your existence will be erased
someone else's life.
your existence will be erased your existence will be erased

your existence will be erased your existence will be erased
do you worry / it will make you feel / like puking up muck all
your existence will be erased your existence will be erased
the time? / how it hurts like horror movies portraying mental
your existence will be erased your existence will be erased
illness as possession? / you must / how you hide your whole
your existence will be erased your existence will be erased
body in a locker / while everyone else showers / they can't
your existence will be erased your existence will be erased
laugh / at what they can't see / right?
your existence will be erased your existence will be erased

wow! this could be a david firth video [bumper 2]

the exorcism of tommy wyatt! (now in black and white)

the only thing evil and needing cast out was a demon, you *could* say, even though it's just your girlskin and painfully90s *poster girl* name, so yeah, sure: you need a fucking exorcism!

(and has your body ever told you how much it wanted to rip out dis-

jointed beams straight from drywall, dreading to find you in the void, in the crawl space? the east thing to do is to become a slug instead: curl up and die haggard and bonedry with a boylean. plus, if others see you like this, they can't commodify you in the zeitgeist, there's nothing interesting to pick at, not even the dried husk of your body. then, if they don't dissect you, how could they know the dimensions of self it housed?)

besides, how are you able to look in the mirror and not recognize yourself? why do the pupils tell on you, how they distend with hellfire? guess you didn't pray enough.

do you yearn for oblivion like children yearn for the mines? [bumper]

how much do you regret suffering? how were you always
threatened with a bad time? when you had access to DIY
ASMR when you booted the computer on to play *Kid Pix 3* in
text so loopy green. you lose yourself in it (really?), sweating, in
that basement (really??) with something so soothing to
probably anyone else? would you ask someone to walk on
eggshells for you for the rest of your life, or are to ready to

do you wish to know what you are looking for? [bumper 1]

the screen cloaks you with night because you looked at it at just the right time. the one in the dark and damp basement, the one on sleep mode, the one adjacent to the lamp that shakes with a wholenote jingle in middle C, someone else is home, huh? the kaleidoscopic green, pixels slowly shifting to black, in WordArt with words only known to AI. with your eyes following it, stimming for extreme situations, think of a dream. think of a really good one [aquatic ambience staticshimmies in] dialed to the sounds of plundering for nightsky stars in the unnaturally dyed water level from *Super Mario 64*, to gray flashing with a bolt of blue on reflective swishy pants, TikToks shrinkwrapping nostalgia with liminal spaces. do this when you need, and you'll wonder why you're always crawling back to the water instead of your mother's arms.

do you wish to know what you are looking for? [bumper 2]

the night cloaks you because you asked it to. fine, does it help to say it takes requests like an open mic? it'll probe you all the same if you wear that chrome bunny suit. it knows you. knows you like a ghost of something that existed before and will exist again. maybe it's not a ghost at all, and time is what sits too heavy in the throat. come on. come the fuck out of there. you can't hide behind a series of statistically improbable events, a metal craft piercing your body with its shiny silver spokes or a birthday that doesn't pass in a ghoulish gray cloud with swooning strobe light so late (or so early?), with what's really happening: the stoking of fear and love with a drugged green gradient. what about this stuff makes you think you're such a bad person? that you should die like Donnie Darko? you know they'll all say, "i feel bad for his family."

what if the phrases "dial up" and "surf's up!" (re)texturize the context? [bumper 1]

answer: pixelated fields of yellow shifting to steelblue waves.

early 2000s internet as a series of chainmail, as popups of *you'll be erased!* and playing *The Sims* in a way that feels like an oedipal reach because your Goth *Sims* file exceeded the maximum quantity of babies in Millennial Gray-tinged and dusty blue bassinets, their big house protruding, and you were cut with luck when the burglar showed up, stealing the ones in the room (trap), or the children choosing to kneel for something else to control them. oepidal (meaning how Freud fucked with the concept of trauma, literally) insofar as rewinding the tape and playing back the parts that make you afraid, the parts that you want to climb into and change. why else do you make it a nightmare? a daydream? any mode of any state of consciousness that is not what it seems?

this poem may predict your future (again), so take with it what you will.

what if the phrases "dial up" and "surf's up!" (re)texturize the context? [bumper 2]

answer: the discography of cacophony electric beats that crashdance in wobbling air.

you're thinking of waves on the beach, don't deny it, and why do you want to be there? bitten all over by weird summer heat, the vibrancy of it all lingers in a hidden way.

like, look when water is streaking the slide that jellos from the impact of body, water not flush but murky enough with dirt creeking all the way to the rim (inflated a bit more in the sun, or maybe it just looks more yellow because of it), your hands cup dense water, neutralsentient and earthy.

what of when the weather shifts to summer quickly this year? how you pull parts of you out of your throat like a clown/magician (are you thinking about playing *The Sims* right now?) gagging on cloth as it pulls out of its mouth in rewind motion. how you trick yourself out of singularity when you are safe for the first time (like, ever in your life)?

this poem may predict your future (again?), so take with it what you will.

let's address the kyle in the room [bumper]

no really. who was he?

because you used to wake up, sundried from hellishly bright and boiling morning light, and say your name was kyle with no shame (at the time). think: what's your name, anyway? and why the fuck isn't it kyle? you wake up the same, hairs sticking up with staticpain, your body

blocked out by polarwhite freakish sun.

and that's what you missed! on tommy... [bumper 1]

find the difference in these "images":

(1) sound in low confidence or sunflowers in the rain [gray lint / static / things fizzing out of a cork / blankness / oblivion / ways to mask dissociation]

(2) white crashing into sky or funneling down the drain [the one fastened on your block, the street you grew up on, or the one where the clown would pull you in, where you think some unknown in multitudes of knowns would present more danger]

does it matter when you'll point to signs to confirm the existence of them? look right here:

(1) quicksilver / teeth / hibernate / in snow / in sleep / grizzly / on the peak / of the mountain / those winters / burgeoning / by rock salt / by sleet / in nights / deprived of sleep

and what does that do for you? will you finally read *Those Winter Sundays* and understand how it manifests in you? or will you buy a free trampoline off Facebook Marketplace and bounce right out of it? which leads to

(2) you're such an unserious person. look, you main as Zero Suit Samus these days. pose for your boyfriend to go from death to dick like a boomerang. text him, *crokay*, [yes!] let it croak out of you, *i said or did it out of fear again, sorry*, it doesn't really matter what it is when you speak, the sound in low confidence.

and that's what you missed! on tommy... [bumper 2]

soft blue sky in broad daylight piles in memories like corrupted MP4 files that have the potential to be restored if you toss your hands up in summer air and feel something radiating warmth into you. and, where are you, really?

1. busy sniffing the tinniness out of plastic octopusing, in the slowest and slimiest movement, to a blaze
2. setting homemade fire drills, in which you save your plushies (the only beings [until your twenties] that respect your needs and consent)
3. pushing you headfirst to haunted in dreams now, really pushing how you can't escape no matter how you parse (drown) yourself
4. because you find yourself here [finally] (now), too. you're typing to your partner over discord before bed: *hon, you're so soft and cute like a plushie.*

and (it's okay) what do you really know?

a half truth and two lies [bumper]

1. you've been sleeping for years, super clear since the late 1990s
2. you read a sign at Blockbuster: *choose torture, fastforward*

the future as an omen [bumper]

see the cat hiding under the bed, pupils sharpening as this predator in the distance mimics her human's voice better than she can chirptrick her way to birds, the way the air wrinkles cries and dissolves them in rain? it's the same as the kid from *Skinamarink* glowering at the pupilpitched darkness under her mother's bed, with nothing but the abyss staring back and a voice cutting through the fugue with, "you know we love you very much," and how much do you blame yourself now for perceived survival, even as you puke it out, even as it possesses you?

sorry, possession is a too heavy charge? it's 2023, you know, *Yellowjackets* is doing it and, like, you're saying you don't have a negapersona that shovels dirt down your throat?, but you do have religious documentaries and *The Exorcist* flickering on a bubbledged screen from 2003, your dad saying he's channel surfing (with static between to prove), and things you dissociate through to survive. you know, the thing you said was "almost fainting" when your parents collectively asked *what was the matter with you, why weren't you listening?* you know that you were doommoding before you could ever form a solid identity? and the charge of possession means you can claim whatever until your voice breaks, everything that makes you strange intensifies like the potential pain from a sunharnessed magnifying glass, as your vision lapses time, as in rewind?

you can walk to Blockbuster, it's okay, it's 2003. you can return the tape now. you'd want to return the tape now, can you imagine the fees if you blink and it's suddenly 2023?

WHO ARE YOU THIS TIME?

contents

these poems have themes of parental trauma, abusive friends, medical trauma, and suicidal ideation

self-help guide to understanding dissociative identity disorder once you reached crisis mode. who are you: tommy, kyle, or josha?

all you've done in bed [all on memorex] +

    as night shifts, its beams twitch beady & yellow [staggering & holographic] +

        how you haunt like a tourist [slipping through dreamland] +

            all pixelated by the glow in stasis like astigmatism [a wish of dissociation distending you] =

what do you choose?

a)   make it feel like a movie you saw in your youth

b)   make yourself flash in the night, without notice like the frequency of high beams triggering deer to camoflage with sky staggering across the starry road

c)   you float in the pool where the soundtrack is canned to dissect reflections from the water, the vicissitude of self(s???)

if you choose *(a)* or *(c)* you are tommy or josha. *go to page 76.*

if you choose *(b)*, you are kyle. *go to page 78.*

as *tommy* or *josha*, you slip in the family room, so invisible, staring into the screen, the glass shivering static with strands of your hair. you hold out your hands for body transference (think: passing trauma to an alter, but nobody consented to contract anything, but that's what happens when there's at least one who wants to commit altercide), but to your dad, it looks a lot like you're a conduit for poltergeists.

sorry, wrong movie.

this time, you asked if children could be possessed, and could it happen to you? (because you never really felt connected to any semblance of a single self, but you didn't have the capacity for imaginary friends.)

so, sorry what?

he will deny what you're asking, hoping you'd never figure anything out (it's best to stay playing the role of *live & fresh* adult captive, for now), anyway. and what would he say when you blink and you're, yet, in another time where your body can only be expressed by others (no, *you* can't touch, or do anything selfsoothing, especially proclivities that decipher confusion via trauma response in repetition).

to when a friend harnesses you with her clammy hands, your mouth open so wide, she can slip her lips onto yours (because, let's be honest, your dissociative delay allows for degradation of quick defense, much like gloom hands heaving goopy muck all over you with its fibrous reach and zaps all of your three hearts ((think: *Tears of the Kingdom*, and how in the present that's all you're playing)). does the night glow loudly, or do you just want to go home? home to where you're trapped all over again, and how many are there still with you, eyes glowing and lunging to the body with hunger, from fear? is it a cycle or the real-life example of the intransitive space-time model?

this time, the tv clicks on, static filling the sphere. wrong input, go figure. but why is it three am, and why is the room tinted with green, and why are wombmoist fleshtoned sacks hugging someone's face on the screen? why does this violation have to happen to the body again and

as *kyle*, you're standing over your bed in
the dead of night, waiting your turn for the
next body tour at the next best place to a
real room, the hospital. you know, the one
with a moodkiller view—

(do you think they haul the unwanted bodies to
bruised earth, pitted then desiccated to sacks
of skin like watermelon left to rot for quite
some time, just like you were and no one had
a clue, especially because you share the same
number as your BMI, which your parents claim
is proof you're a perfectly normal kid. but
guess what? people are always looking in.
maybe this is a threat, maybe someone other
than you should have to worry for once)

are you sleepwalking or are the words
"wish" and "will" regularly used in your
mouth? like the tube spelunking your
throat, descending with bungling velocity;
read: special *doctor's orders* rubber vs.
the punctured chasm puking holograms
of food or bloated air, when a group
of hands hold you down—

(you don't flinch anymore because if the body belongs to anyone, it certainly doesn't belong to you. you've made peace with it, *as in*, will you write your obituary for it and send it snailmail on the last business day of the week because you plan to die on the same day you were born: a monday, unfortunately. or will you look onward, your eyes shriveling to stars, pupils stilted by void that if you get sucked into it, it'll be like you never existed. if you do it, do you think it'll last this time? or will you have to choose all over again?)

traumaspiraling and dissociation as a string of cards from a silent film, character and era unknown

" Double it, and give it to the next person ! "

You say, rubbing your hands on the butchered body suspended from the ceiling

Why don't you stick your head in, try on a new skin ? It's your birth right!

Plus, they're fresh off the hook ! Now, no need to cry...

...When you're green with ill, like when you call a fax line and chatter crunches through

The eye, the front-facing mirror, shattering from noise.

Know there is an Ouija Board printed without " Good Bye"...

A hazard rusted by woods/water, coded in figure and pittered by aquarium

Rocks in piss amber that liquefies from sun, magnifying glass. your left

Retina. void lambasted by perpetuity... This silver screen: Your inheritance. darling!

So / Will you take it. or double it ?

computer reboot method with a dose of sensory deprivation

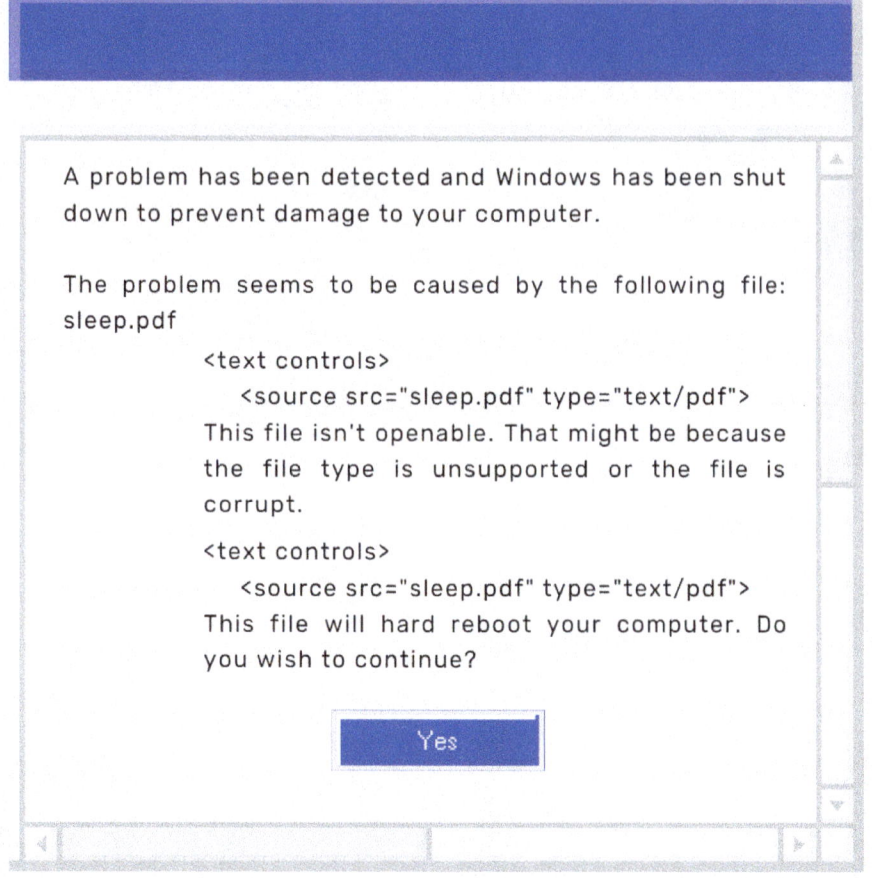

A problem has been detected and Windows has been shut down to prevent damage to your computer.

The problem seems to be caused by the following file: sleep.pdf

<text controls>
<source src="sleep.pdf" type="text/pdf">
This file isn't openable. That might be because the file type is unsupported or the file is corrupt.

<text controls>
<source src="sleep.pdf" type="text/pdf">
This file will hard reboot your computer. Do you wish to continue?

Yes

Runtime error!

Program: C:\WINDOWS\sleep.pdf

The application has requested the Runtime to terminate it in an unusual way. Please open elliott.txt instead.

Ok

```
<text controls>
   <source src="elliott.txt" type="text/txt">
```
To troubleshoot, dissect the screen with a blunt scalpel. A few cuts will do. Feel static travel through the instrument, to your fingers? Let it alter you. You won't feel a single shock if you do it right. Listen to the monotone, gray snow spangle the body. If you want to troubleshoot the feeling, you can always inflict more later. Don't worry yet. All that matters is static worming through you. Did you let yourself unsee it? If you don't know what's happening, is it really happening? Does it matter? The text merges with brightblue computer light not meant for detection. It switches off as you rub your eyes. Night scatters from the scene.

Good morning, Elliott.

checklist: who are you this time? kyle or roman?

kyle	roman
☐ cellar circumsized	☐ commit to the bit start
☐ too purpled to be	☐ an OnlyFans
☐ a hemispherectomy	☐ tell everyone who wants
☐ don't you think?	☐ to own your body
☐ you spill too green	☐ and not have to grapple
☐ to split, so here's to going	☐ with yuckmucky feelings
☐ ghost and how you owe	☐ and the trappings
☐ a little haunting for once	☐ of consent

why does everything go back to a basement fettered with glass tables you look into to conceive a holographic image of yourself, floating in suspension. do you think that shit can be tethered? if so, you're deadwrong, as in you will die if you squeeze us together like the throat of a bird who wronged you (one of you doesn't regret the admission; the threat has been eliminated. why aren't you thanking them, why did you summon them if they can't smash their body into the glass with sudden corporeal form?). maybe it's okay if it happens?

you replicate personalities like a shattered mirror

chrome clouds brazen with venisonblue striates, your body ready to splutter
skydown if you wear your hairsprayed wig so deadblonde and long. whose identity
have you stolen this time, kicking your rubberblack heels into dirt bloated slovenly
from your grift—too many actions one person is capable of doing you might
as well be starrypocked topography, shattering yourself in a glittering of pieces
to foam like seawater and its mist, all things no one will look at, at least not directly
—wrists where we can see them, please, and not in a surveillance way, we
just need to make sure you aren't sculpting the body into a forkedworm
again. waving your tongue as a white flag has more venom to it than you think.
if you prune yourself into the landscape, dirty the stars with grayblue, and
empty the ocean to make way for a tomb, whose name should we write on the headstone?

Thank you to the editors and publications who originally homed these poems:

- "CYOA: scene 3B: LITTLE DANCE, LITTLE DATE" in COLORS: *BLUE*
- "The Vacation: scene 1: DEEPCREEK, MARYLAND VACATION. 2009" in fifth wheel press: *come sail away*
- "The Vacation: scene 4: NOT A CYOA MEMORY, SORRY KID" in Querencia Press: *Summer 2023*
- The second section, *take this quiz! 11 questions to see if you believe courage as a metaphor*, was part of the 2023 Summer Series by Ghost City Press. Individual poems can be found:
  - "happy valentines day? love schadenfreude" in Querencia Press: *Summer 2023*
  - "hey, have you ever considered the word 'rewind' may drop from the next generation's lexicon?" in MAYDAY
- "are you okay with the events currently unfolding? / what's the difference between a game from saw or a nightmare blunt rotation? [bumper 3]" in *body fluids*' substack
- "remember when you picked out your grandma's coffin? [bumper]" in *Eunoia Review*
- "how to fish / how to feel fantastic [bumper 1]" and "how to fish / how to feel fantastic [bumper 2]" in *Fevers of the Mind*
- "when every birthday costumes itself a clown, a spirit halloween opens [bumper]" and "do you wish to know what you are looking for? [bumper 1]" in *manywor(l)ds*
- "the future as an omen [bumper]" in Querencia Press: *Summer 2023*
- "self-help guide to understanding dissociative identity disorder once you reached crisis mode. who are you: tommy, kyle, or josha?" in fifth wheel press: *dreamland*
- "computer reboot method with a dose of sensory deprivation" in Cutbow Quarterly: *Issue 4*
- "you replicate personalities like a shattered mirror" in *moth eaten mag*

This book contains references to Magdalena Bay's *Mercurial World* and Glass Animals' *Dreamland* albums. Specifically, "are you okay with the events currently unfolding? / what's the difference between a game from saw or a nightmare blunt rotation? [bumper 1]" is an acrostic of Magdalena Bay's song "Follow The Leader"; the first line in "a half truth and two lies [bumper]" is from Glass Animals' song "Tangerine".

Thank you to the speakers and workshop leaders of the SAFTA 2023 Trans/Nonbinary Writing Retreat: Ina Cariño, jason b. crawford, Remi Recchia, Nik Buhler, and Emory Night. The workshop inspired the poems "you replicate personalities like a shattered mirror" (ekphrastic of paintings: "Insert" by Martine Syms and "I don't need you to be warm" by Dalton Gata), "is your favorite color blue or are you just sad to see me? / each time you go battery saver mode [bumper]", and "remember when you picked out your grandma's coffin? [bumper]". Thank you to The Sundress Academy for The Arts for hosting this workshop.

Thank you for your support and championing this book: Emily, nat, Sierra, arden, aera, Audrey, and wK. Thank you to my partner and cats for warm nights of slumber and kindness.

www.ingramcontent.com/pod-product-compliance
Lightning Source LLC
Chambersburg PA
CBHW072321180725
29820CB00007B/540